If I Like...

Art and Design

What Job Could I Do?

Cynthia O'Brien

BROWN BEAR BOOKS

Published by Brown Bear Books Ltd
4877 N. Circulo Bujia, Tucson, AZ 85718, USA
and
16 Sun Street, Isleham, CB7 5RT, UK

ISBN 978-1-83572-142-1 (ALB)
ISBN 978-1-83572-148-3 (paperback)
ISBN 978-1-83572-154-4 (ebook)

Library of Congress Cataloging-in-Publication Data available on request

Design Manager: Keith Davis
Children's Publisher: Anne O'Daly
Picture Manager: Sophie Mortimer

Picture Credits
Interior: iStock: DekiArt 20, Georgi Jevic 4, JLco-Julia Amaral 16–17, Aum Racca 6–7, Serbia 10–11, SolStock 12–13; **Shutterstock:** americ181 6, bbernard 8, Chaosamran Studio 17, Estudios Multimeda 5, Gorodenkoff 22, KasePhoto 18–19, Krakenimages.com 14–15, New Africa 20–21, Phoenixns 8–9, Pixel Shot 18, Sithiphong 11, 23, Antonio Truzzi 12, Trzykropy 4–5, Vastram 14.
All other artwork, graphics, and backgrounds: Shutterstock.

Brown Bear Books has made every attempt to contact the copyright holder. If you have any information about omissions, please contact: licensing@brownbearbooks.co.uk

Manufactured in the United States of America
CPSIA compliance information: Batch#5671

Websites
The website addresses in this book were valid at the time of going to press. However, it is possible that contents or addresses may change following publication of this book. No responsibility for any such changes can be accepted by the author or the publisher. Readers should be supervised when they access the Internet.

CONTENTS

Introduction

Art and design jobs are creative. People in these jobs are good at coming up with ideas. They may like drawing or have other artistic skills.

Many people that work in this area are designers. A designer is someone who plans and makes something new. It may be a new piece of jewelry or a new toy. A floral designer makes beautiful things out of flowers.

Designers often work together to come with new ideas.

Content creators combine creative ideas with technical skills.

Top Tech

Some art and design jobs use computer technology. Graphic designers make websites look amazing. Content creators put words, pictures, and videos online.

In the future, creative jobs will include even more exciting technology. Just see where your imagination can take you!

The first artists were cave painters. They painted animals on cave walls more than **65,000** years ago.

Floral designers make arrangements for photo shoots and special events.

Graphic Designer

Graphic designers put pictures and words together. They use their creative skills to get information across.

This may be a book, a magazine, or a website. Graphic designers also create ads, posters, and other reports. Different kinds of businesses hire designers. These include book publishers and ad companies. Other designers are freelance. Companies hire them for projects.

Graphic designers create new logos for companies and brands.

A Designer at Work

Most graphic designers use computers to make their designs. They may draw ideas as well. Designers need a good understanding of color and shape.

Writers supply designers with words. Graphic designers decide how the words should look. They find the right images to go with them. These may be photographs or drawings or videos.

Become a Graphic Designer

High school classes help designers build a portfolio. Classes may be in art or website design. Next, it is a good idea to have a diploma in graphic design. This helps to build skills. Some graphic designers intern to learn on the job.

TOOLS OF THE TRADE

Computer

Drawing tablet

Sketchbook

Pencils

Toy Designer

A toy designer thinks of new toys to make. Trucks, stuffed animals, and action figures are all types of toys.

There are outdoor toys, musical toys, and other kinds. Some toys make learning fun. Many toys use technology. Toy companies hire designers. Some toy designers work on their own. They sell their ideas to a toy company. The company makes the toy and sells it.

Some toys are made of wood. The designer decides which material is best to use.

Playing with Ideas

Toy design starts with a good imagination. Toy designers draw their ideas on paper. They also use computer drawing tools. They decide how the toy should look, move, or sound.

Many toy designers make models of their ideas. They may use a 3D printer. This printer makes a real object from a computer design.

TOOLS OF THE TRADE

Sketchbook

Pencils

Computer

3D printer

Become a Toy Designer

Some colleges offer degrees in toy design. People can also get a degree or diploma in art or graphic design. These programs may include courses in toy design. Students should build a portfolio of their toy ideas. After college, it is a good idea to intern at a company.

Content Creator

A content creator makes fun or interesting things to share online. These can be videos, photos, or podcasts.

Some content creators are influencers. An influencer shares content on social media. A lot of people see it. A fashion influencer may model clothes in a video. This can make other people want to buy the clothes.

There are about **200 million content creators** around the world.

Become a Content Creator

Content creators do not need a degree or diploma. However, it is helpful to take courses in content creation. A content creator should build a good portfolio of their work. This shows that they can put together amazing content.

Putting It Together

Many content creators share what they love. Someone who likes to cook may post online cooking classes. Someone who loves movies might share reviews.

Some content creators work for a company. They help sell the company's products. Other creators work on their own. They might promote their own products.

Content creators often use a smartphone to film and edit their videos.

TOOLS OF THE TRADE

Video camera

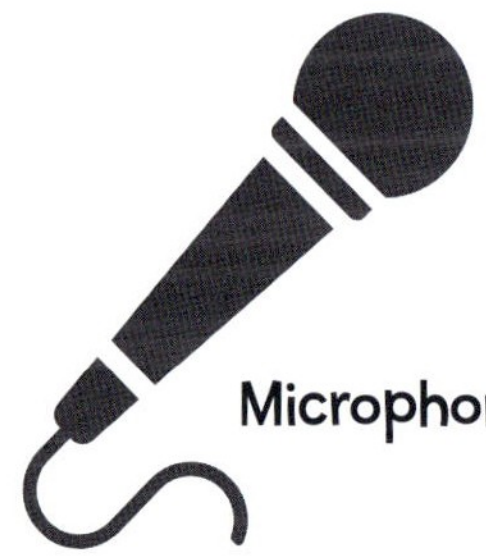

Microphone

Lighting

Computer

Textile Designer

Textile designers are fabric artists. They make textiles look fun and beautiful.

Textile designers create new textiles. They come up with colors and patterns. They work with different materials, including wool or cotton. Textile designers often work in fashion, designing cool clothes. Others may work in furniture or in industry.

A sample is a small piece of material.

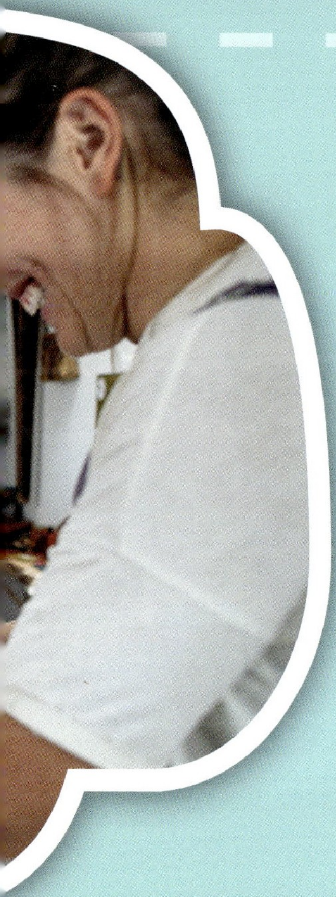

New Ideas

Textile designers draw their ideas and use computers to help them. They may make a sample to see how it looks.

Textile designers look for ideas. They look at nature and paintings. They see what colors and patterns are popular. Textile designers also think about how fabrics will be used. Fabric on car seats needs to be strong. Dress fabrics may be thin and silky.

Become a Textile Designer

Most textile designers have a degree in textile design. Some take a fashion or graphic design program. If they do this, they still need special courses in textiles. They learn how textiles are made. They also learn design skills.

TOOLS OF THE TRADE

Computer

Sketchbook

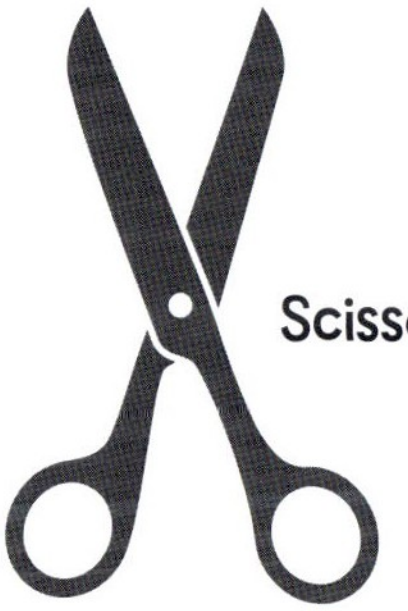

Scissors

Fabric

Floral Designer

A floral designer is an artist who works with flowers and plants. They put them together in amazing arrangements.

Floral designers decorate spaces. They understand how different flowers work together. They have a good sense of color and shape. Many floral designers work for stores. Some designers have their own business.

Designers may make sculptures from flowers.

Art with Flowers

Floral designers use fresh flowers and plants in new ways. A client may ask for certain types of flowers. They may want particular sizes or colors.

Floral designers create arrangements for weddings and other special events. They put together backgrounds for magazine photographs or ads.

TOOLS OF THE TRADE

Flowers and plants

Secateurs

Ribbons

Ball of string

Become a Floral Designer

Floral designers do not need a degree. They do need to learn about different flowers and plants. They must understand how to keep them healthy. Many designers start out by working for a florist or garden center. They build a portfolio by creating arrangements and taking photographs.

Floriography is the language of flowers. It is the idea that different flowers have special meanings.

Jewelry Designer

Earrings, bracelets, and necklaces are kinds of jewelry. A jewelry designer comes up with new styles.

Many designers make the jewelry themselves. A buyer may ask a designer to create a special piece just for them. Some designers give their designs to a jewelry maker. This happens for large jewelry companies. The company makes many copies of the same design.

Become a Jewelry Designer

Many jewelry designers have a degree or certificate from an art college. They take courses to learn metal working and other skills. They learn about different jewels and how to use them.

Making Jewelry

Jewelry designers work in different materials. Many designers use metals, such as silver. Some designers make jewelry from recycled plastic or leather. They may carve patterns into the materials.

Materials can be shaped, too. A jewelry designer may use a wax model for metal jewelry. Designers pour the melted metal into the model. They take the wax off after the metal hardens.

Jewelry designers draw their design by hand or use a computer.

TOOLS OF THE TRADE

Pliers

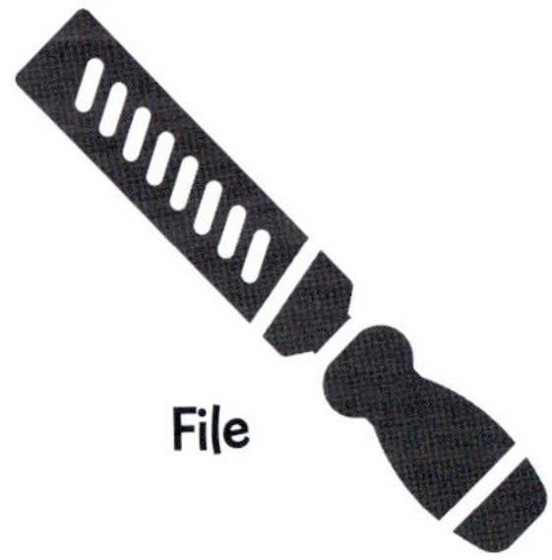

File

Magnifying visor

Landscape Designer

Landscape designers make outdoor spaces beautiful and healthy.

Designers work for landscaping companies. Some work for city governments or at a garden center. People hire landscape designers to design backyards. Designers also create plans for fun areas like parks and playgrounds.

A designer makes a plan to show how a space will look and what plants will grow there.

Living Art Spaces

Landscape designers create a plan to show their client. They suggest flowers and trees for the space. They think about the soil and the sunlight.

Designers think about the environment. Planting more trees cleans the air. The designers suggest features such as pathways. Usually, other people do the planting and building. Designers oversee the work.

TOOLS OF THE TRADE

Computer

Camera

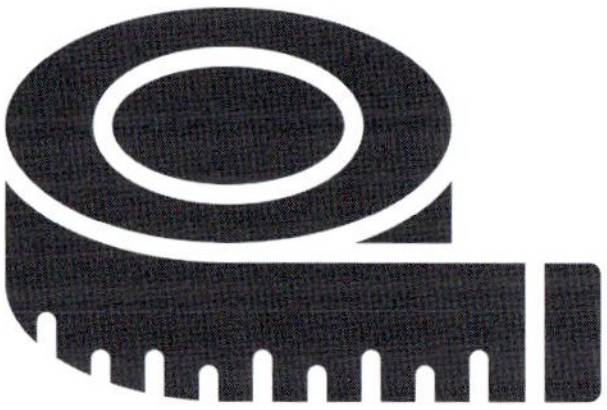

Measuring tools

Become a Landscape Designer

After high school, landscape designers earn a diploma. They learn about plants and develop skills in design. New designers need hands-on experience. They also need a portfolio. Often, they intern with a landscaping firm to get experience.

Landscape designers helped make the High Line in New York. This **1.45-mile** (2.3 km) park used to be a railway line.

Makeup Artist

A makeup artist uses cosmetics. They create special looks for people's faces or bodies.

Some people want makeup done for a wedding or special event. Makeup artists often work on actors and models. They work in salons, theaters, and movie studios. Many makeup artists are freelance. They work in clients' homes or where they are needed.

A theater makeup artist designs makeup for stage performances.

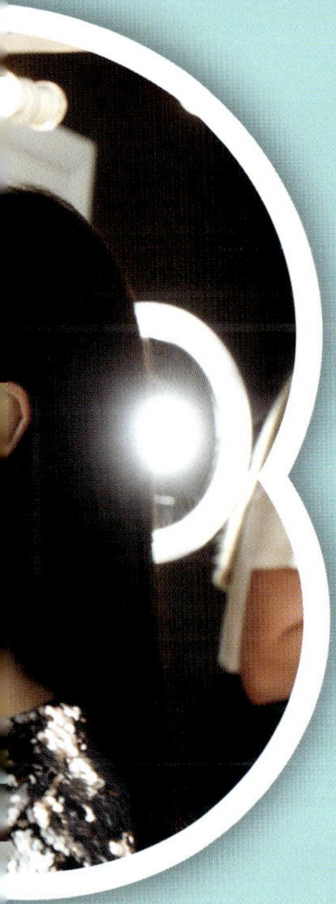

A New Look

Before each job, a makeup artist meets with the client. They find out what they need. A bride may want a glamorous look. A model may need a dramatic look for an advertisement. Actors often need makeup to look like the characters they play.

Makeup artists work with brushes, sponges, and other tools. They apply colors and textures. Theater actors need special stage makeup that lasts longer than regular cosmetics.

TOOLS OF THE TRADE

Powders

Creams

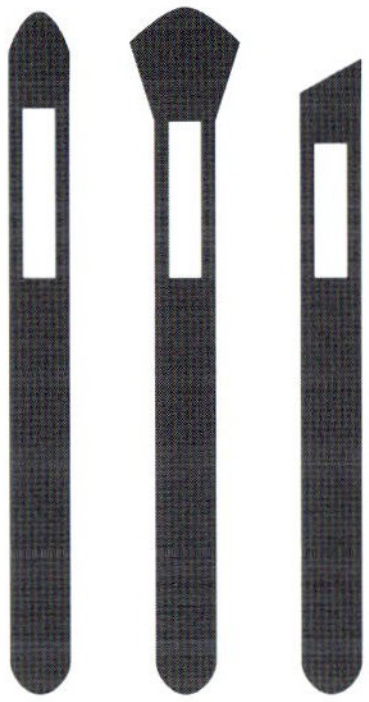

Brushes

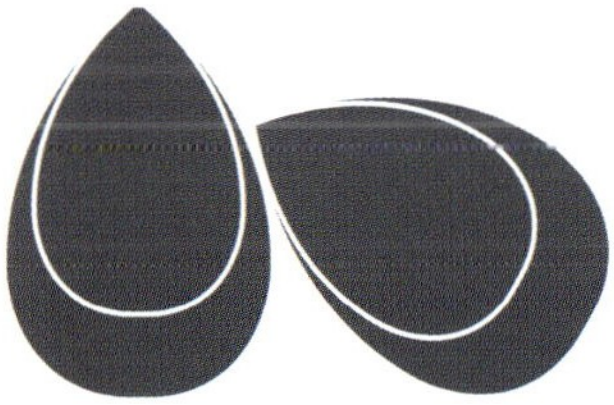

Sponges

Become a Makeup Artist

Some high schools offer classes in makeup. There are also online courses. It is a good idea to get a college certificate. A college makeup program teaches skills. Students learn about special effects. In some places, makeup artists also need a license.

AI Artist

AI artists use computers to make art.

In the future, more AI artists will create art for galleries. Others will work for ad companies. AI artists think of ideas. Then they work with a computer. They tell the computer what they want. The computer uses AI to make an artwork. It looks through lots of different images. The artist can use the artwork or make changes.

An AI art system may look through **5.85 billion** images to make a new artwork.

Become an AI Artist

It is helpful to get a degree in AI art or design. Students learn design skills. They also learn how to use AI technology. This helps them get a job making AI art.

Glossary

AI (artificial intelligence) technology that lets computers solve problems and learn in a similar way to humans

apprentice a person who trains under a licensed or certified person

client someone who pays for the services of someone else

cosmetics beauty products people use such as lipstick, nail polish, and creams

creative able to make or do something new or with imagination

floral having to do with, or made up of, flowers

intern to work with and learn from an experienced person

logo a symbol or design that represents a company or brand

portfolio a collection of a person's work, such as drawings

textures the feel or look of a surface, such as rough or smooth

Find Out More

Books

Amin, Anita Nahta. *The Business of Being a Style Influencer*. Capstone, 2021.

Olsen, Elsie. *AI and the Arts*. Lerner, 2025.

Reeves, Diane Lindsey. *Create and Experience*. Cherry Lake, 2025.

Websites

kids.britannica.com/kids/article/designer/611151

pbslearningmedia.org/resource/graphic-designer-video/job-pop/

pbslearningmedia.org/resource/landscape-designer-video/job-pop/

Index